Sally

Surprise Garden

Sally lived in an upstairs apartment.
She wanted a garden.

2

"Gary has carrots in his garden," Sally said.
"He had one for lunch today."

4

"We can't have a garden like Gary,"
Mom said. "But you could grow
something in a pot."

6

Sally and Mom went to the plant store.
Mom got a big pot and a bag of soil.
Sally chose the seeds.

"What seeds did you get?" Mom asked.

"It's a surprise," Sally said.

9

Sally filled the pot with soil.
She put it by the window
and planted her seeds.

10

After a while, some green shoots came up

"What are they?" Mom asked.

"It's a surprise," Sally said.

12

Sally watered her garden,
and soon there were lots of green leaves
She picked some.

"Wait for the flowers," Mom said.

"I'm not growing flowers," Sally said.

"It's lettuce," Sally said.
"I'm making a salad.
Do you want some?"

16